ANGELS
ON
EARTH

THEY ARE WAITING ON YOU

by
Michael P. Jacobs

rockhousepublishing
sellersburg • indiana

Angels on Earth; They Are Waiting On You
ISBN 13: 978-0-97198-350-2
ISBN 10: 0-97198-350-X
Copyright © 2002 by Michael P. Jacobs
4224 Mel Smith Road
New Albany, Indiana 47150

Published by Rock House Publishing
1718 Sterling Oaks Drive
Sellersburg, IN 47172
www.rockhousepub.com

DEDICATION

I dedicate this book to my father, Jack Jacobs, who loved me and walked in integrity before me all the days of his life. To my mother, Joyce Jacobs, who loved God and prayed me through my drug addiction days into the family of God. My mother taught me to trust God and love people. It's with my deepest respect and honor I dedicate this book to my parents, Mr. and Mrs. Jack H. Jacobs.

PREFACE

Forty-seven years ago was my first understanding that angels are on the earth with us. I was five years old and awakened from sleep. I went to the bedroom window and looked out. About twelve to fifteen feet away stood a being. He was white in color and partially transparent. An energy or power was emanating from him in waves. I was in such awe, I ran to wake my mother who came to the window and saw this being also. Years later I understand that God wants us to know that these beings are present here on the earth to help us.

FOREWORD

Throughout 35 years of ministry, I have seen the results of the angels at work with me in the ministry entrusted to me. They have protected my life, brought provision into my hands, joined my path with the right people, and have worked with me in the healing ministry.

Although we don't worship angels, we must not overlook or neglect the much-needed supply they bring to our lives and ministries. Psalm 103:20 tells us that the angels hearken unto the voice of His word. As we speak the word of God, they meet those words and work with us in the earth.

When Pastor Jacobs began sharing with me the revelation he has received on angels, I told him, "This has to get out to the body of Christ!" So, I'm thankful to see these truths reach your life because we all need greater knowledge of these *"...ministering spirits, sent forth to minister for them who shall be heirs of salvation."* (Hebrews 1:14)

Dr. Ed Dufresne
Ed Dufresne Ministries

INTRODUCTION

In the Bible, people had situations that only an encounter with an angel could bring them out of or into. Is it true that angels are only "working behind the scenes" and we have little or nothing to do with their activities? I believe that God is endeavoring to get some things over to us about angels.

Part of the reason we've had so little operation and manifestation of angelic activity on the earth is because we've had very little teaching and much of it has been in error.

We must begin to realize that these creatures are listening to our words. Our words and behavior must agree with God's covenant to activate their ministry fully.

Angels have a specific purpose and ministry to carry out. All the angels have divine things to do, but they don't all do the same things. Some have directions to give, provisions to bring, or other assignments to fulfill.

They are all different. They have different degrees of glory or anointing and they are in different classes. Notice how almost every time they appeared to a human being in the Bible, they say, "Fear not." Why? The angels of the Bible are masculine, strong, and powerful to look upon. The angels also need us to stay in faith for them to minister to us fully. When we are in fear, we open the door to the devil. When we walk by faith in God's word, this opens the door for angelic ministry.

One of the most important things to know is that angels are not involved with us to entertain us.

They are not here to socialize with us. People talk, believe, and act like angels are fat little babies with beer-bellies and curly hair, but we know from the scripture these things are not true.

In these last days, things are changing quickly. God is elevating his church, his ministers, and his people to a place we have never known before. It's time for signs, wonders, healings, and demonstrations. Both the old and new covenants indicate that signs and wonders come, at least in part, through the ministry of angels. Jesus needed and valued their help and so do we.

I pray this book will cause faith to come to your hearts concerning the angels assigned to you and your ministries.

TABLE OF CONTENTS

Chapter One

GIVING THE MORE EARNEST HEED

It was 1983 and I was scheduled to teach a three-day conference on the subject of angels. The church I was attending at the time had always been supportive of my ministry and even provided a small room in one of their buildings as an office and place of prayer.

As I was praying in this office before the first service of the conference, suddenly a whole multitude of angels came into the room. Here I was surrounded by a group of beings that to me looked like runners at the start of a marathon. There was a tangible intensity and eagerness in their demeanor. Before I could really determine what was happening, one of them stepped forth and began to speak to me, saying, "We are so excited that you're teaching about us, for we've desired to be involved in the body of Christ and they won't let us." After this message was delivered the angel doing the speaking stepped back into the group and they vanished.

I was left in a little room with a big assignment. I realized the thrust of the message delivered to me from that short encounter was going to be a major part of my ministry from that point on. The message? The angels wanted to be involved in our lives but something was hindering their activity. I have found over and over again that a lack of knowledge in any area of the Word will hinder the benefit or ministry of that Word from being a reality to us. I can say with confidence that this applies to the ministry of angels as well.

"Therefore we ought to give the more earnest heed to the things which we have heard, lest at any time we should let them slip."
(Hebrews 2:1)

Hebrews chapter two follows the discourse in Hebrews one on the supremacy of Jesus and the covenant He established. I am not taking anything away from that, but rather showing how Hebrews one reveals a lot of information about angels, culminating in the fourteenth verse...

"Are they (angels) not all ministering spirits, sent forth to minister for them who shall be heirs of salvation."

You know that the text of the Bible is God inspired but men added the chapter numbers to aid us in locating verses. I am on solid ground in saying that one of the major things we are being told not to let slip is the ministry of angels. We ought to take heed to that. Not only just heed, doesn't the scripture say, "earnest heed?" We ought to give the more earnest heed. It's like an emphasis on top of emphasis to tell us to pay attention to this area of our inheritance.

I want to tell you something; I grew up in church from age five to fifteen. I was at church every Sunday. I was at church for vacation Bible school. I never heard one message on angels ever, period! I left church at the age of fifteen and went out into the world. I found plenty of stuff out there in the supernatural realm. Believe you me, I got in the midst of it, and it's real.

By the age of 21, I had become a drug addict and was living in California. One of the supernatural experiences I had during this time was at a seance. A good friend of mine had a demon speak through his mouth imitating the voice of a lady that we had known who had died just a few months before. I'm telling you that we got over in the supernatural.

In December of 1971, I was saved and went back to the church I grew up in. I was there for five more years and still never heard a message on angels. In 1976 I attended a two-year Bible school that is a part of a prestigious seminary. I think they might have sold one book on angels at the seminary bookstore, but it didn't have much in it that I could use. They didn't have any course dedicated to teaching on angels and I don't remember angels being discussed in any course I had.

The Bible says; ... ***"give the more earnest heed to the things which we have heard, lest at any time we should let them slip" (Hebrews 2:1).*** I had no information concerning angels to heed or let slip. Unfortunately this is very typical of so many that go to church and claim to be believers. We are believers and we're to believe the scriptures, especially when we are told to pay earnest heed to something.

Chapter Two

WHAT ANGELS ARE REALLY LIKE

Most records of even secular history have references to some kind of supernatural creatures or beings in their literature. Of course, some of it is off center and not based on truth, Jesus said the Word of God is truth, *"Sanctify them through thy truth: thy Word is truth" (John 17:17)*. There's hardly a civilization that doesn't have something in it about some kind of spiritual activity or being. Sometimes it's God and sometimes it's not. All spiritual activity is to be judged by the Word of God.

So, what are angels really like? First of all, angels are created beings.

> *"Praise ye him, all his angels: praise ye him, all his hosts, Let them praise the name of the Lord: for he commanded, and they were created." (Psalm 148:2, 5)*

What does this mean to you? Well, it means that angels are not your dead relatives. An angel has never been a human and a human will not become an angel. Man is created in a different class than that of angels. Man is created in the image of God - angels are not.

Another characteristic of angels is that God created and designed them with specific purposes and ministries. The word "angel" in the Greek and Hebrew is the word "messenger or sent one". Angels are spirit beings...

> *"And of the angels he saith, Who maketh*
> *his angels spirits, and his ministers a flame*
> *of fire" (Hebrews 1:7)*

As spirit beings, they normally operate in the spirit world or unseen world.

> *"Who is the image of the invisible God, the*
> *firstborn of every creature: for by him were*
> *all things created, that are in heaven, and*
> *that are in earth, visible and invisible,*
> *whether they be thrones, or dominions, or*
> *principalities, or powers: all things were*
> *created by him, and for him"*
> *(Colossians 1:15-16).*

There are visible and invisible beings on the earth and some of them are angels.

In the ministry of Elisha we have an example of beings that were present but unseen to the natural eye. It wasn't until his spiritual eyes were opened that Elisha's servant knew the reality of their presence, although they were already there in the spirit.

> ...*"And he answered, fear not: for they that*
> *be with us are more than they that be with*
> *them. And Elisha prayed, and said, Lord, I*
> *pray thee, open his eyes, that he may see. And*
> *the Lord opened the eyes of the young man;*
> *and he saw: and, behold, the mountain was*
> *full of horses and chariots of fire round about*
> *Elisha" (2 Kings 6:8-17)*

Elisha made a significant point when he said, "they that be with us are more than they that be with them." This should give us a real sense of security knowing that all around us are angels sent to assist and protect us.

Something else to know about angels is that each one has a name. Hebrews 1:4 says, ***"Being made so much better than the angels, as he hath by inheritance obtained a more excellent name than they."*** For Jesus' name to be more excellent, all the angels would have to have names for the name of Jesus to be compared to. For example, Gabriel, Michael, and Lucifer are some names that we are given in the scriptures to identify angels.

Angels experience joy.

> ***"Likewise, I say unto you there is joy in the presence of the angels of God over one sinner that repenteth," (Luke 15:10)***

This would indicate the angels have the ability to experience a certain level of emotions or feelings.

Angels speak languages.

> ***"Though I speak with the tongues of men and of angels, and have not charity, I am become as sounding brass, or a tinkling cymbal" (1 Corinthians 13:1)***

Angels can communicate with us and also with one another.

> ***"And the angel of the Lord protested unto Joshua, saying, Thus saith the Lord of hosts; If thou wilt walk in my ways, and if thou wilt keep my charge, then thou shalt also***

> *judge my house, and shalt also keep my*
> *courts, and I will give thee places to walk*
> *among these that stand by."*
> *(Zechariah 3:6-7)*

> *"Above it stood the seraphims: each one had*
> *six wings; with twain he covered his face,*
> *and with twain he covered his feet and with*
> *twain he did fly. And one cried unto another,*
> *and said, Holy, holy, holy, is the Lord of*
> *hosts: the whole earth is full of his glory."*
> *(Isaiah 6:2-3)*

These particular angels were communicating with one another.

Angels are holy.

> *"Whosoever therefore shall be ashamed of*
> *me and of my words in this adulterous and*
> *sinful generation; of him also shall the Son*
> *of man be ashamed, when he cometh in the*
> *glory of his Father with the holy angels."*
> *(Mark 8:38).*

> *"And they said, Cornelius the centurion, a*
> *just man, and one that feareth God, and of*
> *good report among all the nation of the Jews,*
> *was warned from God by an holy angel to*
> *send for thee into his house, and to hear*
> *words of thee" (Acts 10:22)*

The elect angels of God walk in holiness before God and carry out their assignments on earth as holy beings.

Angels are mighty in strength. They are not the fat, beer-bellied, feminine looking creatures depicted in figurines, pictures and Christmas cards.

> *"Bless the Lord, ye his angels, that excel in strength, that do his commandments, hearkening unto the voice of his word"*
> *(Psalm 103:20)*

In appearance angels are awesome and generate fear in those who see them, which is why they say "fear not".

> *"In the end of the Sabbath, as it began to dawn toward the first day of the week, came Mary Magdalene and the other Mary to see the sepulcher. And behold, there was a great earthquake: for the angel of the Lord descended from heaven, and came and rolled back the stone from the door, and sat upon it. His countenance was like lightning, and his raiment white as snow: and for fear of him the keepers did shake, and became as dead men. And the angel answered and said unto the women, Fear not ye: for I know that ye seek Jesus, which was crucified,"*
> *(Matthew 28:1-5)*

Pilate had put his best and bravest soldiers to watch the tomb, yet when the angel appeared to them they fainted for fear.

Angels can communicate with men.

> *And there appeared unto him an angel of the Lord standing on the right side of the*

altar of incense. And when Zacharias saw him, he was troubled, and fear fell upon him. But the angel said unto him, Fear not, Zacharias: for thy prayer is heard; and thy wife Elisabeth shall bear thee a son..."
(Luke 1:11-13)

This is just one of many references where an angel communicated with men and women in the earth.

Angels can appear as human beings.

"Then there came again and touched me one like the appearance of a man, and he strengthened me. And said, O man greatly beloved, fear not: peace be unto thee, be strong, yea, be strong. And when he had spoken unto me I was strengthened, and said, let my Lord speak; for thou hast strengthened me", (Daniel 10:18-19). "Be not forgetful to entertain strangers: for thereby some have entertained angels unawares",
(Hebrews 13:2)

As spirit beings, angels never die. Jesus said in Luke 20:36; *"Neither can they die any more: for they are equal unto the angels..."* This is a significant fact because it means that every angel listed in scripture is still available today to minister to and for us.

Angels can visibly appear or they can operate invisibly. You don't have to see an angel to receive the benefits from them. In the book of Acts it says that the angel spoke to Philip.

> *"And the angel of the Lord spake unto
> Philip, saying, Arise, and go toward the
> South unto the way that goeth down from
> Jerusalem unto Gaza, which is desert,"*
> *(Acts 8:26)*

It doesn't indicate that he appeared to Philip. Now he could have appeared to Philip, but it doesn't say he did. The passage says the angel spoke. We know the Holy Ghost speaks from within us. An angel speaks from the outside and your spirit picks it up. It's in the realm of the spirit but a different operation than being led by the Spirit.

Concerning angels, and on any spiritual subject, our final authority cannot be men's ideas or even their "spiritual experiences".

> *"We have also a more sure word of prophecy;
> whereunto ye do well that ye take heed, as
> unto a light that shineth in a dark place,
> until the day dawn, and the day star arise in
> your hearts: knowing this first, that no
> prophecy of the scripture is of any private
> interpretation. For the prophecy came not
> in old time by the will of man: but holy men
> of God spake as they were moved by the Holy
> Ghost"* *(2 Peter 1:19-21)*

The more sure Word of prophecy refers to the written Word of God. Let's stay with the "more sure word" of prophecy especially in this arena where there is so much speculation and misinformation.

Chapter Three

CLASSES OF ANGELS

There are many different kinds of beings listed in scripture. For the purposes of this book, we are interested in the elect angels, those angels that are working for us and with us. It is important to note that angels have different ministries. Just as there are different ministries among men, such as the apostle, prophet, evangelist, pastor and teacher. There are differences of ministries among the angels, (i.e.) archangels, seraphim, cherubim, and guardians.

In both men and angels the ministries may be different but with the same purpose, that is ministering to and for God and man.

> *"But to which of the angels said he at any time, sit on my right hand, until I make thine enemies thy footstool? Are they* (the angels) *not all ministering spirits, sent forth to minister for them who shall be heirs of salvation?" (Hebrews 1:13-14)*

With that in mind, let's go into some detail on the different classes of angels and the differences in their ministries.

CHERUBIM

Cherubim are the first class of angels mentioned in the Bible.

> *"So he drove out the man; and he placed at the east of the garden of Eden cherubims,*

*and a flaming sword which turned every way,
to keep the way of the tree of life."
(Genesis 3:24)*

These beings were put there to keep man from getting back in the garden and eating of that tree, which would have kept him eternally lost with no hope of redemption. I think we can draw a conclusion that part of angelic ministry in general is to keep us out of certain places for our protection.

Cherubim are described in detail in Ezekiel 10:1-22.

"Then I looked, and, behold, in the firmament that was above the head of the cherubims there appeared over them as it were a sapphire stone, as the appearance of the likeness of a throne. And he spake unto the man clothed with linen, and said, go in between the wheels, even under the cherub, and fill thine hand with coals of fire from between the cherubims, and scatter then over the city. And he went in in my sight. Now the cherubims stood on the right side of the house, when the man went in; and the cloud filled the inner court. Then the glory of the Lord went up from the cherub, and stood over the threshold of the house; and the house was filled with the cloud, and the court was full of the brightness of the Lord's glory. And the sound of the cherubims' wings was heard even to the outer court, as the voice of the almighty God when he speaketh. And it came to pass, that when he had commanded the man clothed with linen, saying, take fire from

between the wheels, from between the cherubims; then he went in, and stood beside the wheels. And one cherub stretched forth his hand from between the cherubims unto the fire that was between the cherubims, and took thereof, and put it into the hands of him that was clothed with linen: who took it, and went out. And there appeared in the cherubims the form of a man's hand under their wings. And when I looked, behold the four wheels by the cherubims, one wheel by one cherub, and another wheel by another cherub: and the appearance of the wheels was as the colour of a beryl stone. And as for their appearances, they four had one likeness, as if a wheel had been in the midst of a wheel. When they went, they went upon their four sides; they turned not as they went, but to the place whither the head looked they followed it; they turned not as they went. And their whole body, and their backs, and their hands, and their wings, and the wheels were full of eyes round about, even the wheels that they four had. As for the wheels,

---

"I THINK WE CAN DRAW A CONCLUSION THAT PART OF ANGELIC MINISTRY IN GENERAL IS TO KEEP US OUT OF CERTAIN PLACES FOR OUR PROTECTION."

---

it was cried unto them in my hearing, O wheel. And every one had four faces: the first face was the face of a cherub, and the second face was the face of a man, and the third the face of a lion, and the fourth the *face of an eagle. And the cherubims were lifted up. This is the living creature that I saw by the river of Chebar. And when the cherubims went, the wheels went by them: and when the cherubims lifted up their wings to mount up from the earth, the same wheels also turned not from beside them. When they stood, these stood; and when they were lifted up, these lifted up themselves also: for the spirit of the living creature was in them. Then the glory of the Lord departed from off the threshold of the house, and stood over the cherubims. And the cherubims lifted up their wings, and mounted up from the earth in my sight: when they went out, the wheels also were beside them, and every one stood at the door of the east gate of the Lord's house; and the glory of the God of Israel was over them above. This is the living creature that I saw under the God of Israel by the river of Chebar; and I knew that they were the cherubims. Every one had four faces apiece, and every one four wings; and the likeness of the hands of a man was under their wings. And the likeness of their faces was the same faces which I saw by the river of Chebar, their appearances and themselves: they went every one straightforward."*

It is interesting to note the appearance of some of these creatures. They have four faces, four wings, and under their wings the appearance of human hands. Each class of angels is unique. They are equipped differently for their particular function.

The cherubim have a ministry of protecting holy things. In the book of Exodus, God instructed Moses to design two cherubim of gold to cover the mercy seat in the holy of holies.

"And thou shalt make two cherubims of gold, of beaten work shalt thou make them, in the two ends of the mercy seat. And make one cherub on one end, and the other cherub on the other end: even of the mercy seat shall ye make the cherubims on the two ends thereof. And the cherubim shall stretch forth their wings on high, covering the mercy seat with their wings, and their faces shall look one to another; toward the mercy seat shall the faces of the cherubim be. And thou shalt put the mercy seat above upon the ark; and in the ark thou shalt put the testimony that I shall give thee. And there I will meet with thee, and I will commune with thee from above the mercy seat, from between the two cherubim which are upon the ark of the testimony, of all things which I will give thee in commandment unto the children of Israel." (Exodus 25:18-22)

God told Moses to make everything in the tabernacle after the pattern in heaven.

"Who serve unto the example and shadow of heavenly things, as Moses was admonished of God when he was about to make the tabernacle: for, see, saith he, that thou make all things according to the pattern shewed to thee in the mount." (Hebrews 8:5)

So, these gold statues that Moses made on the earth have a living counterpart in the heavenly tabernacle.

> *"And the temple of God was opened in heaven, and there was seen in his temple in the ark of his testament: and there were lightnings, and voices, and thunderings, and an earthquake, and great hail."*
> *(Revelation 11:19)*

The book of Second Samuel tells us that God rode upon a cherub and did fly.

> *"He bowed the heavens also, and came down; and darkness was under his feet. And he rode upon a cherub, and did fly: and he was seen upon the wings of the wind."*
> *(2 Samuel 22:10-11)*

It would appear that God has charged cherubim with special assignments that other angels aren't equipped to do.

The next example of a cherub seems to bear out this fact.

> *"Thou art the anointed cherub that covereth; and I have set thee so: thou wast upon the holy mountain of God; thou hast walked up and down in the midst of the stones of fire."*
> *(Ezekiel 28:14)*

Most Bible scholars agree that this is speaking of Lucifer before his fall. Here again we see cherubim involved with holy things and holy places.

ARCHANGELS

"Arch" is the word that means a chief or a principal one. That would be one who has some authority, would it not? Look in Revelation 12:7...

> *"and there was war in heaven: Michael and his angels..."*

Michael is a chief or principal one among the angels. Michael, as an archangel, is over other angels under his authority. Michael is the only angel mentioned in scripture specifically as an archangel and is referenced again in the book of Jude vs. 9.

> *"Yet Michael the archangel..."*

While we see that Michael is the only Archangel called by name in scripture, the Bible does make reference to other archangels.

> *"But the prince of the kingdom of Persia withstood me one and twenty days: but, lo, Michael, one of the chief princes, came to help me; and I remained there with the kings of Persia." (Daniel 10:13)*

Notice it reads "...one of the chief princes..." meaning there must be others. We are not told specifically how many there are.

It is significant to note that Michael is always defending, fighting, or assisting others in these things. In Revelation 12:7...

> *"And there was war in heaven: Michael and his angels fought against the dragon: and the dragon fought and his angels,"*

in verse 8,

"and prevailed not."

It is encouraging to know that not only do we win as believers, but that the angels assigned to help us win too.

SERAPHIM

The next group of Angels we will discuss are called seraphim. The seraphim's first ministry is worship to God. In the Hebrew language the word seraphim means, "burning ones". Isaiah 6:1-8 is the only place in the Bible they are named and the only place that gives any detail about them.

> *"...In the year that king Uzziah died I saw also the Lord sitting upon a throne, high and lifted up, and his train filled the temple."*

This is a vision of heaven. Isaiah the prophet saw the Lord on a throne and his train, or his robe, filled this temple.

> *"Above it stood the seraphims: each one had six wings."*

Remember the cherubim had four wings, now these creatures have six wings.

> *"With twain he covered his face, and with twain he covered his feet, and with twain he did fly."*

This is a very unusual looking being, if you can imagine it in your mind.

"And one cried unto another, and said, holy, holy, holy, is the Lord of hosts" (the Lord of the armies, the Lord of the angelic beings) *"the whole earth is full of his glory, and the posts of the door moved at the voice of him that cried, and the house was filled with smoke."*

We see these beings had tremendous power in their voices where they could make the posts of the door move at their cry. Nothing weak or effeminate about these creatures! Smoke or incense represents intercession, worship, and prayer in the Bible. The house was filled with smoke, which would indicate that there was prayer, worship and praise or a combination of these things happening in the heavenly temple. These creatures are holy. There are all different kinds of things going on up in heaven that affects this planet.

"And another angel came and stood at the altar, having a golden censer; and there was given unto him much incense, that he should offer it with the prayers of all saints upon the golden altar which was before the throne. And the smoke of the incense which came with the prayers of the saints, ascended up before God out of the angel's hand. And the angel took the censer, and filled it with fire of the altar, and cast it into the earth: and there were voices, and thunderings, and lightnings, and an earthquake."
(Revelation 8:3-5)

Reading on in Isaiah 6:5...

"Then said I, woe is me! For I am undone."

You know when you see the Lord and you begin to see His glory that's the first thing that will dawn on you, how undone you are. I know that sometimes when I get in the presence of God, He puts his finger right on the pulse of what I need. "You need to straighten that attitude out and you need to deal with this in your life." One of the first things He usually deals with is my mouth. How about you? And so here's Isaiah and he said,

> *"Woe is me. I'm undone, for I'm a man of unclean lips..."*

That just means he was not speaking right and he knew it.

> *"And I dwell in the midst of a people of unclean lips: for mine eyes have seen the king, the Lord of hosts. Then flew one of the seraphims unto me, with a live coal in his hand, which he had taken with the tongs from off the altar: and he laid it upon my mouth."*

This seraphim has hands coming out from underneath his wings with which he used tongs to take a coal from the altar and placed it on Isaiah's lips.

> *"He laid it on my mouth, and said, lo, this hath touched thy lips; and thine iniquity is taken away, and thy sin purged."*

He's using an angel to cleanse Isaiah's communication.

As we get in God's presence as a church, the angels assist us in ministry to man.

"And he shewed me Joshua the high priest standing before the angel of the Lord, and Satan standing at his right hand to resist

"THIS CHARGE, WHEN KEPT, WOULD GIVE HIM PLACES TO WALK AMONG THE ANGELS."

him. And the Lord said unto Satan, the Lord rebuke thee, O Satan; even the Lord that hath chosen Jerusalem rebuke thee: is not this a brand plucked out of the fire? Now Joshua was clothed with filthy garments, and stood before the angel. And he answered and spake unto those that stood before him, saying, take away the filthy garments from him. And unto him he said, behold, I have caused thine iniquity to pass from thee, and I will clothe thee with change of raiment. And I said, let them set a fair mitre upon his head. So they set a fair mitre upon his head, and clothed him with garments. And the angel of the Lord stood by. And the angel of the Lord protested unto Joshua, saying, thus saith the Lord of hosts; if thou wilt walk in my ways, and if thou wilt keep my charge, then thou shalt also judge my house, and shalt also keep my courts, and I will give thee places to walk among these that stand by."
(Zechariah 3:1-7)

Joshua the priest was ministered to by the Lord through an angel and given a charge by the Lord of Hosts. This charge, when kept, would give him places to walk among the angels. Angelic ministry will be manifest around us as we keep God's Word and walk in His ways.

GUARDIAN ANGELS

In the book of Daniel, it is stated that there are watchers watching us. The Hebrew word for watcher in these scriptures is the word guardian.

> *"I saw in the visions of my head upon my bed, and, behold, a watcher and an holy one came down from heaven; this matter is by the decree of the watchers, and the demand by the word of the holy ones: to the intent that the living may know that the most high ruleth in the kingdom of men, and giveth it to whomsoever he will, and setteth up over it the basest of men. And whereas the king saw a watcher and an holy one coming down from heaven, and saying, hew the tree down, and destroy it; yet leave the stump of the roots thereof in the earth, even with a band of iron and brass, in the tender grass of the field; and let it be wet with the dew of heaven, and let his portion be with the beasts of the field, till seven times pass over him."*
> *(Daniel 4:13, 17, 23)*

The word guardian, according to Webster's dictionary, is "one who has care of a person or property of another; protector; to protect from danger or preserve." I'm sure if you think back on your life, you will remember a time when something tragic almost happened but at the last minute you were delivered. Most, if not all, of these circumstances were changed for your benefit through the ministry of guardian or personal angels assigned to you. When you see the president or a leader of some country, you have noticed the men or women guarding them. They are always looking and discerning what might need to be done to protect the person they are assigned to. It's the same in the world of the spirit. Thank God you and I have a spiritual "secret service". Though they are rarely seen, yet they are tremendously effective. These beings (angels) are assigned to deliver you from evil plots of the enemy (devil).

> *"The angels of the Lord encampeth round about them that fear him, and delivereth them." (Psalm 34:7)*

> *"He delivereth me from mine enemies: yea, thou liftest me up above those that rise up against me: thou hast delivered me from the violent man." (Psalm 18:48)*

The patriarch Jacob, when blessing his grandsons before his departure, makes this comment...

> *"The angel which redeemed me from all evil, bless the lads; and let my name be named on them, and the name of my fathers Abraham and Isaac; and let them grow into a multitude in the midst of the earth." (Genesis 48:16)*

He declares plainly that the angel assigned to him had redeemed or delivered him from all evil. Jacob had a guardian angel assigned to protect and preserve him and so do we. When you add the thought coming from the latter part of verse 15, *"all my life long"*, you can understand even more that this angel was with him "all his life long". I'm convinced this is one reason he had a long life. Also, in Psalm ninety-one verse ten and eleven, the psalmist declares God assigns angels to people personally.

> *"There shall no evil befall thee, neither shall any plague come nigh thy dwelling. For he shall give his angels charge over thee, to keep thee in all thy ways." (Psalms 91:10-11)*

Father God gives guardian angels charge over you. Notice carefully Psalm ninety-one verse sixteen.

> *"With long life will I satisfy him, and shew him my salvation." (Psalm 91:16)*

Guardian angels and long life go together as we learn about angels, believe for their protection and learn what activates their ministry for us. Jesus also had something to say about guardian angels being assigned to you personally.

> *"Take heed that ye despise not one of these little ones; for I say unto you, that in heaven their angels do always behold the face of my father which is in heaven." (Matthew 18:10)*

In referring to small children, Jesus said they had angels assigned to them. "Their angels" implies angels directly assigned to an individual. The word "heaven" does not mean the actual location of heaven as much as the realm of the spirit. In other words, the angel assigned to you and your children is in tune with Father and His desires for you. The guardian angel assigned to you is here on earth.

Jesus had a personal angel assigned to Him in the earth also.

"I Jesus have sent mine angel to testify unto you these things in the churches. I am the root and the offspring of David, and the bright and morning star." (Revelation 22:16)

Remember what Jesus said about children and "their" angels? It's interesting to note that Jacob (Genesis 48:16) and Jesus did not need their guardian angels on earth once they left the planet. This indicates again the importance of their ministries to us as guardians while we are here on earth.

When Peter was set free from prison in Acts 12, he was delivered through the ministry of an angel.

"Peter therefore was kept in prison: but prayer was made without ceasing of the church unto God for him. And when Herod would have brought him forth, the same night Peter was sleeping between two soldiers, bound with two chains: and the keepers before the door kept the prison. And, behold, the angel of the Lord came upon him, and a light shined in the prison: and he smote Peter on the side, and raised him up, saying, Arise up quickly. And his chains fell off from his hands. And the angel said unto him, Gird thyself, and bind on thy sandals. And so he did. And he saith unto him, Cast thy garment about thee, and follow me. And he went out, and followed him; and wist not that it was true which was by the angel; but thought he saw a vision. When they were past the first and the second ward, they came unto the iron gate that leadeth unto the city; which opened

to them of his own accord: and they went out, and passed on through one street; and forthwith the angel departed from him. And when Peter was come to himself, he said, Now I know of a surety, that the Lord hath sent his angel, and hath delivered me out of the hand of Herod, and from all the expectation of the people of the Jews. And when he had considered the thing, he came to the house of Mary the mother of John, whose surname was Mark; where many were gathered together praying. And as Peter knocked at the door of the gate, a damsel came to hearken, named Rhoda. And when she knew Peter's voice, she opened not the gate for gladness, but ran in, and told how Peter stood before the gate. And they said unto her, Thou art mad. But she constantly affirmed that it was even so. Then said they, It is his angel", (Acts 12:5-15)

He went to John Mark's house and those praying there began to declare it is "his angel". It's evident from this statement that the church of the New Testament had teaching and sound doctrine concerning angels assigned to people personally.

Chapter Four

ANGELS ON EARTH

There *are* angels in heaven but many are ministering on the earth now. This is their main place of habitation and operation, not heaven. There are over 300 references in the Bible to angels. In approximately 100 of those references, angels appeared and ministered to people on this planet.

Let's look at what is traditionally called "Jacobs ladder". This account is found in Genesis 28:12.

> *"And he dreamed, and behold a ladder set up on the earth"*, (I want you to mark this in your thinking; *"on the earth"*) *"and the top of it reached to heaven..."*

In other words, God didn't throw a rope out from heaven to the earth. This ladder started at earth and went up. Let's read...

> *"and behold the angels of God ascending and descending on it,"*

...not descending and ascending. Now, let's go to verse 16 and 17.

> *"And Jacob awaked out of his sleep, and he said, surely the Lord is in this place; and I knew it not. And he was afraid, and said, how dreadful* (or awesome) *is this place! This*

is none other but the house of God and this is the gate of heaven."

According to the New Testament the house of God is the church.

"...That you may know how to behave yourself in the house of God, which is the church of the living God, pillar and ground of the truth." (1 Timothy 3:15)

Isn't that right? And Jacob also said, *"this is the gate of heaven" (Genesis 28:17).* Did you know the church is the gate of heaven? Heavenly things flow through the church out into the world, out into the community, and out into the nations.

Another scripture concerning the habitation and location of some of the angels is John 1:51, Jesus said...

"...Verily, verily, I say unto you, hereafter you shall see heaven open, and the angels of God ascending and descending upon the son of man."

Notice the phrase, *"ascending and descending upon the son of man."* This is in total agreement with what Jacob saw in his dream, it's the same order, ascending and descending.

There is a large contingency of angels on the earth. Now let's go to Zechariah 1:7-10.

"Upon the four and twentieth day of the eleventh month, which is the month Sebat, in the second year of Darius, came the Word of the Lord unto Zechariah, the son of

Berechiah, the son of Iddo the prophet, saying, I saw by night, and behold a man riding upon a red horse, and he stood among the myrtle trees that were in the bottom; and behind him were there red horses, speckled, and white. Then said I, O my Lord, what are these? And the angel that talked with me said unto me, I will show thee what these be. And the man that stood among the myrtle trees answered and said, these are they whom the Lord hath sent to walk to and fro through the earth."

Now these three passages; Genesis 28:12-17, John 1:51, and Zechariah 1:7-10 specify the place of assignment for certain angels. Many of them are on the earth. They're down here with us. We're talking about angels on the earth.

The Bible says even more concerning angels on earth.

"For I think that God hath set forth us the apostles last, as it were appointed to death: for we are made a spectacle unto the world, and to angels, and to men."
(1 Corinthians 4:9)

If you have a good reference Bible, the word "spectacle" there in the footnote is the Greek word "theater". Now what do you do when you go to a theater? You listen and look. That's what the angels are doing right now, listening and looking. The book of Daniel, chapter 4, verses 13, 17, and 23, says the angels are called watchers; holy ones come down from heaven. They're watchers. They're watching us. They're here with us today in the earth. They're watching you right now.

They are watching you in church.

> *"Keep thy foot when thou goest to the house of God, and be more ready to hear, than to give the sacrifice of fools: for they consider not that they do evil. Be not rash with thy mouth and let not thine heart be hasty to utter anything before God: for God is in heaven and thou upon earth: therefore let thy words be few." (Ecclesiastes 5:1-2)*

We've already established that the house of God is the church. Read verse 6,

> *"Suffer not thy mouth to cause thy flesh to sin; neither say thou before the angel, that it was an error: wherefore should God be angry at thy voice, and destroy the work of thine hands?"*

Now God is not destroying things, but what it's saying here is, you're talking contrary to the covenant and He's not able to protect you fully like He wants to. This passage indicates the angel was in the congregation's presence and their talking was before him. When we gather together in an assembly, a conference, prayer meeting, or any other function as the church, the angels are with us, and are listening to our words.

First Timothy 5:21 tells us this concerning specific functions of the ministry Paul addressed in this 5th chapter.

> *"I charge thee before God, and the Lord Jesus Christ, and the elect angels, that thou observe these things without preferring one*

before another, doing nothing by partiality."

It's evident the angels are observing these functions. Verse 22 goes on to talk about ordination or setting someone apart for ministry by the laying on of hands.

> *"Lay hands suddenly on no man, neither be partaker of other men's sins: keep thyself pure," (1 Timothy 5:22)*

The elect angels are present for ordination and even specifically assigned to the ministry being set apart or ordained.

Having considered all these references, Hebrews 12:22-24 takes on new meaning.

> *"But ye are come unto Mount Sion, and unto the city of the living God, the heavenly Jerusalem, and to an innumerable company of angels, to the general assembly and church of the first born, which are written in heaven, and to God the judge of all, and to the spirits of just men made perfect, and to Jesus the mediator of the new covenant, and to the blood of sprinkling, that speaketh better things than that of Abel."*

We have access to these things now. Angels are included.

Chapter Five

ANGELS IN WORSHIP
AND INTERCESSION

According to the Word of God, angels have a place in worship and intercession.

> *"And I saw in the right hand of him that sat on the throne a book written within and on the backside, sealed with seven seals. And I saw a strong angel proclaiming with a loud voice, who is worthy to open the book, and to loose the seals thereof? And no man in heaven, nor in earth, neither under the earth, was able to open the book, neither to look thereon. And I wept much, because no man was found worthy to open and to read the book, neither to look thereon. And one of the elders saith unto me, weep not: behold, the lion of the tribe of Juda, the root of David, hath prevailed to open the book, and to loose the seven seals thereof. And I beheld, and, lo, in the midst of the throne and of the four beasts, and in the midst of the elders, stood a lamb as it had been slain, having seven horns and seven eyes, which are the seven Spirits of God sent forth into all the earth. And he came and took the book out of the right hand of him that sat upon the throne. And when he had taken the book, the four beasts and*

four and twenty elders fell down before the lamb, having every one of them harps, and golden vials full of ordours, which are the prayers of saints. And they sung a new song, saying, Thou art worthy to take the book, and to open the seals thereof: for thou wast slain, and hast redeemed us to God by thy blood out of every kindred, and tongue, and people, and nation; And hast made us unto our God kings and priests: and we shall reign on the earth. And I beheld, and I heard the voice of many angels round about the throne and the beasts and the elders: and the number of them was ten thousand times ten thousand, and thousands of thousands; saying with a loud voice, worthy is the lamb that was slain to receive power, and riches, and wisdom, and strength, and honour, and glory, and blessing" (Revelation 5:1-12)

We can clearly see the Lord says there are beasts and many angels around the throne in heaven. They are actively involved *"saying with a loud voice, worthy is the lamb..."* These angels are lifting their voices in worship to the lamb. Let's look at another open window into a heavenly scene.

"And when he had opened the seventh seal, there was silence in heaven about the space of half an hour. And I saw the seven angels which stood before God; and to them were given seven trumpets. And another angel came and stood at the altar, having a golden censer; and there was given unto him much incense, that he should offer it with the

prayers of all saints upon the golden altar which was before the throne. And the smoke of the incense which came with the prayers of the saints, ascended up before God out of the angel's hand. And the angel took the censer, and filled it with fire of the altar, and cast it into the earth: and there were voices, and thunderings, and lightnings, and an earthquake." (Revelation 8:1-5)

Through this window that is open into the spirit for us, we see much activity that takes place in heaven. Our prayers and intercessions come up before the throne. An angel then adds incense to our prayers. Then the prayers with the incense ascend up before God. The angel then gets fire from off the altar and puts it in his censer. He then casts these prayers, incense and fire into the earth where we are and live. The results are "voices", thunderings, lightnings and an earthquake.

Back in 1971, I was a drug addict living in a tenement house in Venice Beach, California. I had gone into the bathroom to shoot up some drugs when I had a vision and a voice spoke to me and said, "Michael come home." I know now my mother and others were praying for me to be delivered from my lifestyle. Thank God my mother prayed and God added His fire from heaven. I

"WE CAN CLEARLY SEE THE LORD SAYS THERE ARE BEASTS AND MANY ANGELS AROUND THE THRONE IN HEAVEN. THEY ARE ACTIVELY INVOLVED..."

---

heard a "voice". I went back home to Ohio and within six weeks I was born again. Praise God for the angels, which have their place in bringing prayers and results together. Remember these results were manifested in the earth after the angel cast his censer in the earth.

Heaven is waiting on you to pray, worship and intercede. Give the angels something to work with. When you give God your voice in worship and intercession, He will release his voice in the earth.

Chapter Six

WHAT ANGELS DO

ANGELS PROTECT US

"For he shall give his angels charge over thee, to keep thee in all thy ways."
(Psalm 91:11)

We know from Psalm 91 that they are sent and God has charged them to keep us in all our ways, for those who dwell under the shelter of the most high God and those who will say...

"There shall no evil befall thee, neither shall any plague come nigh thy dwelling. For he shall give his angels charge over thee, to keep thee in all thy ways. They shall bear thee up in their hands, lest thou dash thy foot against a stone. Thou shalt tread upon the lion and adder: the young lion and the dragon shalt thou trample under feet."

Here the angels have a charge to keep us. God has charged them and we are the recipients of their protection.

"The angel of the Lord encampeth round about them that fear him, and delivereth them." (Psalm 34:7)

I found out in the Hebrew language that the word delivereth means wholly and to deliver fully. In 1980 I was pastoring a a rural city. My neighbor at the time was demon possessed and attacked me verbally and threatened to break my nose. He also had a pistol hanging out of his back pocket. He drew his fist back to hit me and was restrained by an invisible force. As I stood there, the Lord spoke to me and said, "Your angel is here with you and no one will be harmed." My wife, holding our baby daughter, was also standing close by. I'm so thankful for the Lord's protection through these ministering spirits. The angels allowed us to escape wholly and delivered us fully from a very dangerous situation.

Angels can defend you.

> *"Behold, I send an angel before thee, to keep thee in the way, and to bring thee into the place which I have prepared. Beware of him, and obey his voice, provoke him not; for he will not pardon your transgressions: for my name is in him... But if thou shalt indeed obey his voice, and do all that I speak; then I will be an enemy unto thine enemies, and an adversary unto thine adversaries. For mine angel shall go before thee, and bring thee, ...and I will cut them off."*
> *(Exodus 23:20-23)*

I like the fact if I'm walking with God, He's going to be an enemy to my enemies. The angels begin to defend and surround us as we reverence God. They will encamp round about us and defend us.

> *"Plead my cause, O Lord, with them that strive with me: fight against them that fight*

against me. Take hold of shield and buckler, and stand up for mine help. Draw out also the spear, and stop the way against them that persecute me: say unto my soul, I am thy salvation. Let them be confounded and put to shame that seek after my soul: Let them be turned back and brought to confusion that devise my hurt." (Psalm 35:1-4)

While I was in Mexico with missionary Mike Hrabal several years ago, I received a call from my wife, Diana. She was at our church for vacation Bible school and said someone had come in the church parking lot the night before and drawn pentagrams and put lit candles around. She said all of the children seemed upset, so I prayed with her and took authority over the devil. My wife then went to each classroom pleading the Blood of Jesus over them. When she did that, all the confusion stopped immediately! Some of the ladies that were serving in the VBS said "You know, whenever you began to plead the Blood of Jesus, everything calmed right down."

The devil tries to seek your hurt, and he seeks after your soul to confuse you. All we have to do is stand on the covenant.

"...let them be as chaff before the wind."
(Psalm 35:5)

That means there is no substance to them.

"And let the angel of the Lord chase them."

Do you know the angels can chase?

(v 6) "And their way be dark and slippery:

and let the angel of the Lord persecute them.
(v 7) "For" (this is the key) *"without cause*
they have hid for me their net in a pit, which
without cause they have digged for my soul."

In other words if you are innocent, you didn't do anything and the devil is trying to attack you, you ought to stand on that verse. I have stood on that before.

"Let the angels of the Lord chase them. Let
their way be dark and slippery."

I'm talking about evil powers that are trying to operate against you. The angels fight and defend us. The enemy, your enemies, way becomes dark and slippery. We are not fighting flesh and blood. We're not talking directly about people but rather evil spiritual forces that motivate them.

ANGELS BRING US DELIVERANCE

Peter is in jail in Acts 12:5-15 and they are going to execute him.

"Peter therefore was kept in prison: but
prayer was made without ceasing of the
church unto God for him. And when Herod
would have brought him forth, the same night
Peter was sleeping between two soldiers,
bound with two chains: and the keepers
before the door kept the prison." (vs 5-6)

They had him in tight security.

"Behold, the angel of the Lord came upon
him, and a light shined in the prison." (v 7)

Nobody turned the light on, but the angel had light coming off him.

> *"And he smote Peter on the side, and raised him up, saying, arise up quickly. And his chains fell off from his hands."*

Angels are involved in liberating people.

> *"And the angel said unto him, gird thyself, and bind on thy sandals. And so he did. And he saith unto him, cast thy garment about thee, and follow me. And he went out and followed him; and wist not that it was true which was by the angel; but thought he saw a vision. When they were past the first and the second ward, they came unto the iron gate that leadeth unto the city; which opened to them of his own accord."* *(vs 8-10)*

Doors are opening automatically; chains are falling off people.

> *"and they went out, and passed on through one street; and forthwith the angel departed from him. And when Peter was come to himself, he said, now I know of a surety, that the Lord hath sent his angel, and hath delivered me out of the hand of Herod..."*
> *(v 10)*

> *"And they said unto her, thou art mad. But she constantly affirmed that it was even so. Then said they, it is his angel."* *(v 15)*

Why would they say that? Now there must be something in the

New Testament that would indicate that they had a teaching or a doctrine about angels being assigned to you? Why else would they say, *"It is his angel?"*

Now if you thought back on your life, most could stand up and give testimony about almost getting shot, almost getting in a bad accident, almost drowning, almost something. Then at the last minute, there you were on the other side of it and you were preserved. I was teaching on angels years ago, and a man told me that he was driving around a curve one day and the door flew open and his daughter slid out in mid air and stayed there. All of a sudden, something threw her back in the car and shut the door. I've preached on angels all around this country and in many other countries. I always have several people come and tell how they were preserved by supernatural intervention.

ANGELS HELP DURING TEMPTATION

> *"And turning the cities of Sodom and Gomorrha into ashes condemned them with an overthrow, making them an ensample unto those that after should live ungodly; and delivered just Lot, vexed with the filthy conversation of the wicked: (For that righteous man dwelling among them, in seeing and hearing, vexed his righteous soul from day to day with their unlawful deeds;) the Lord knoweth how to deliver the godly out of temptations, and to reserve the unjust unto the day of judgment to be punished."*
> *(2 Peter 2:6-9)*

The angels can help you in a time of temptation. They delivered Lot in that situation. (Read Genesis 19:1-16). They ministered to

Jesus in Luke 22:40-43.

> *"And when he was at the place, he said unto them, Pray that ye enter not into temptation. And he was withdrawn from them about a stone's cast, and kneeled down, and prayed, saying, Father, if thou be willing, remove this cup from me: nevertheless not my will, but thine, be done. And there appeared an angel unto him from heaven, strengthening him."*

Jesus was in the garden praying, and it says an angel came and strengthened him. It doesn't tell us how, but Daniel 10:18-19 tells us that an angel touched him one time, and he was strengthened (v 18). And in verse 19 the angel spoke to Daniel, and he was strengthened.

> *"Then there came again and touched me one like the appearance of a man, and he strengthened me. And said, O man greatly beloved, fear not: peace be unto thee, be strong, yea, be strong. And when he had spoken unto me, I was strengthened, and said, Let my lord speak; for thou hast strengthened me",* *(Daniel 10:18-19)*

We know from comparing scripture with scripture that this angel either touched Jesus or he spoke to Jesus in the garden of Gethsemane. We know that was a real test and trial for Jesus. Jesus was praying the pressure was on, and it was some strong pressure and temptation there. If Jesus received and accepted their ministry and needed their help, shouldn't we?

> *"And he was there in the wilderness forty*

*days, tempted of Satan; and was with the wild
beasts; and the angels ministered unto him,"
(Mark 1:13)*

We're not told how they ministered. We know from the Bible
that angels can bring food. (Read 1 Kings 19:1-8). We know
from the Bible that they can lay hands on people at times because
they did Daniel. We know they can speak something that would
encourage a person at a time like that. The angels came and they
ministered unto Jesus as a man. That's encouraging to me. If the
two most trying times in Jesus' life angels were involved in providing
some assistance or some relief or some kind of help, wouldn't it
stand to reason that if Jesus needed their assistance, I would need
it also?

ANGELS EXECUTE JUDGMENT FOR GOD

*"Which is a manifest token of the righteous
judgment of God, that ye may be counted
worthy of the kingdom of God, for which ye
also suffer: Seeing it is a righteous thing
with God to recompense tribulation to them
that trouble you; And to you who are
troubled rest with us, when the Lord Jesus
shall be revealed from heaven with his
mighty angels, In flaming fire taking
vengeance on them that know not God, and
that obey not the gospel of our Lord Jesus
Christ: Who shall be punished with
everlasting destruction from the presence of
the Lord, and from the glory of his power."
(2 Thessalonians 1:5-9)*

These angels are going to come and they are going to take

vengeance. The whole book of Revelation is filled with this aspect of angels bringing judgment. It's going to be poured out on this planet. Thank God we are delivered from the wrath to come.

"And to wait for his son from heaven, whom he raised from the dead, even Jesus, which delivered us from the wrath to come."
(1 Thessalonians 1:10)

In Acts 12:22 King Herod stood up and the people said...

"...he's a god, and he speaks with the voice of a god..."

In other words, they were honoring him as a god. He didn't rebuke them. He didn't set it straight. He didn't say, "I'm just a man," which he should have said. The angels smote him and he died. Do you remember when Peter came to Cornelius? He fell down to worship Peter because he'd had an angelic visitation. He grabs Peter around the feet and Peter said, "Stand up. I'm a man just like you."

ANGELS REVEAL THINGS TO US

"There was a certain man in Caesarea called Cornelius, a centurion of the band called the Italian band, a devout man, and one that feared God with all his house, which gave much alms to the people, and prayed to God alway. He saw in a vision evidently about the ninth hour of the day an angel of God coming in to him, and saying unto him, Cornelius. And when he looked on him, he was afraid, and said, What is it, Lord? And

he said unto him, Thy prayers and thine alms are come up for a memorial before God. And now send men to Joppa, and call for one Simon, whose surname is Peter: He lodgeth with one Simon a tanner, whose house is by the sea side: he shall tell thee what thou oughtest to do." (Acts 10:1-6)

This is the story of Cornelius. He was an Italian man and a soldier. A devout man who feared God with his entire house. And the angel came and appeared to him. The angel revealed to him how to get hold of this man Simon Peter.

"He'll come and he'll tell you words whereby you will be saved."

Cornelius had need of someone to tell him how to get saved. God sent an angel to him and revealed to him to send for somebody who could bring the gospel message to him.

Now there's revelation knowledge that comes out of studying the Bible, but sometimes angels bring a revelation or a word of knowledge to someone. Joseph had three different dreams that God gave him. In the first one the angel said, "Marry this woman. It's okay."

"But while he thought on these things, behold, the angel of the Lord appeared unto him in a dream, saying, Joseph, thou son of David, fear not to take unto thee Mary thy wife; for that which is conceived in her is of the Holy Ghost," (Matthew 1:20)

Then he had another dream where an angel came and said, "Get into Egypt."

> *"And when they were departed, behold, the*
> *angel of the Lord appeareth to Joseph in a*
> *dream, saying, Arise, and take the young*
> *child and his mother, and flee into Egypt,*
> *and be thou there until I bring thee word:*
> *for Herod will seek the young child to destroy*
> *him," (Matthew 2:13)*

Then he went down into Egypt, and he had a dream down in Egypt and the angel said, "come back now into Israel."

> *"But when Herod was dead, behold, an angel*
> *of the Lord appeareth in a dream to Joseph*
> *in Egypt, saying, Arise, and take the young*
> *child and his mother, and go into the land of*
> *Israel: for they are dead which sought the*
> *young child's life." (Matthew 2:19-20)*

The angels can reveal all kinds of things to us. Where to go or where not to go, who we need to get a hold of that can speak something we need to hear. Many times in the last few years the angels have come and said we want to minister with you in this service. Usually there's something specific they want to assist in, many times in the area of healing or miracles.

ANGELS ASSIGNED TO MINISTERS

> *"I charge thee before God, and the Lord*
> *Jesus Christ, and the elect angels, that thou*
> *observe these things without preferring one*
> *before another, doing nothing by partiality.*
> *Lay hands suddenly on no man, neither be*

partaker of other men's sins: keep thyself pure." (1 Timothy 5:21-22)

The Apostle Paul is talking about ordaining ministers, laying on of hands, and setting people apart for ministry. In verse twenty-one, he talks about God the Father, the Lord Jesus Christ and the elect angels. Notice angels are right in the midst of these holy services that we call ordination.

In the Old Testament prophets, the ministry of Jesus, and the early church, we see angels around all of these as they carry out their ministries. Usually it was not a one-time event, but continually the angels were ministering with them and around them on an on going basis.

"WOULD IT NOT MAKE SENSE THAT SPECIFIC ANGELS ARE ASSIGNED TO OUR MINISTRIES?"

Would it not make sense that specific angels are assigned to our ministries? We, as ministers, do not all have the same mission and anointing. However, all of us in ministry are called to walk in the supernatural. Angels are a part of our inheritance, our calling, and the supernatural that we are called to. Some men will have healing ministries, teaching and preaching ministries and many other ministries. Would it not seem right that God assigns angels with certain characteristics, which fit with those that have specific ministries? We need to consider these things more intensely, lest we let these things slip.

"Are they not all ministering spirits, sent forth to minister for them who shall be heirs of salvation? Therefore we ought to give the more earnest heed to the things which we

have heard, lest at any time we should let them slip." (Hebrews 1:14 - Hebrews 2:1)

ANGELS AND PROSPERITY

First of all, let's establish the fact that God wants you to prosper.

"Praise ye the Lord. Blessed is the man that feareth the Lord, that delighteth greatly in his commandments. Wealth and riches shall be in his house: and his righteousness endureth for ever." (Psalm 112:1, 3)

"Beloved, I wish above all things that thou mayest prosper and be in health, even as thy soul prospereth." (3 John 2)

Of course, your prosperity is tied to your giving and your faith. The angels, however, have a direct bearing on your prosperity. We know from the word of God that all angels have ministries and are called to minister. There are angels assigned to us as covenant people, which are equipped and anointed to help us prosper. I certainly realize that prosperity can be in different ways such as material, mental, and physical. However, I'm specifically talking here about material and financial prosperity.

"Bless the Lord, ye his angels, that excel in strength, that do his commandments, hearkening unto the voice of his word. Bless ye the Lord, all ye his hosts; ye ministers of his, that do his pleasure."
(Psalm 103:20-21)

We can clearly see from these verses the angels are ministers of

God and they do His pleasure. If we knew what the Lord's pleasure is from His word, we know the angels are involved in that process also.

> *"Let them shout for joy, and be glad, that favour my righteous cause: yea, let them say continually, Let the Lord be magnified, which hath pleasure in the prosperity of his servant." (Psalm 35:27)*

If the Lord has pleasure in the prosperity of His servants under the old covenant, how much more would He take pleasure in the prosperity of His sons and daughters under the new covenant?

Let's look at an example of someone prospering with the assistance of an angel. Abraham commissions his servant to find a wife for his son Isaac.

> *"But thou shalt go unto my father's house, and to my kindred, and take a wife unto my son. And I said unto my master, Peradventure the woman will not follow me. And he said unto me, the Lord, before whom I walk, will send his angel with thee, and prosper thy way; and thou shalt take a wife for my son of my kindred, and of my father's house: And he said unto them, Hinder me not, seeing the Lord hath prospered my way; send me away that I may go to my master." (Genesis 24:38-40, 56)*

Angels can help by giving direction in your life, by bringing you into contact with the right people. Real prosperity from God comes to us in all the realms in which we exist: spirit, soul and body. One of the most precious ways in which God blesses us is to find the right mate for our life. God blessed Abraham's servant in helping to find Rebekah and bring her back.

> *"Who can find a virtuous woman? For her price is far above rubies. The heart of her husband doth safely trust in her, so that he shall have no need of spoil."*
> *(Proverbs 31:10-11)*

Chapter Seven

ANGELS AND ORDER

Angels like order. If your life is in disorder, they do not like it. Strife and confusion may quench the ability of angels to work for you.

> *"For God is not the author of confusion, but of peace, as in all churches of the saints,"* and *"Let all things be done decently and in order."* (1 Corinthians 14:33, 40)

You know peace should be a significant thing to look for in your life to know that you are in the right place.

Having things in order is imperative for your life. I'm talking about the Word bringing divine order to us. I'm talking about spiritual fathers and pastors bringing balance in our lives — divine order.

When you begin to think maturely, you are going to be thankful that somebody is watching over your life that has spiritual sense. You are going to be very grateful that they take the initiative to correct you. You will be thankful when they say, " Listen, I don't know about this or that"...or "Maybe you need to go pray a little more", or "I don't think that's a good idea." Instead of being irritated or upset, we should thank God someone is taking an interest in our life and ministry.

"What do you mean by order?" I mean living according to the scriptures, living upright before God; having the right attitude about

---

those over us in the Lord.

> *"Remember them which have the rule over you, who have spoken unto you the Word of God: whose faith follow, considering the end of their conversation. Obey them that have the rule over you, and submit yourselves: for they watch for your souls, as they that must give account, that they may do it with joy, and not with grief: for that is unprofitable for you." (Hebrews 13:7, 17)*

The glory of God came when the tabernacle was built according to the pattern or divine order as instructed by God.

> *"Who serve unto the example and shadow of heavenly things, as Moses was admonished of God when he was about to make the tabernacle: for, see, saith he, that thou make all things according to the pattern shewed to thee in the mount." (Hebrews 8:5)*

> *"Then a cloud covered the tent of the congregation, and the glory of the Lord filled the tabernacle." (Exodus 40:34)*

When we get things in divine order, the glory comes. The angels are a part of the glory and they like divine order.

> *"In the year that king Uzziah died I saw also the Lord sitting upon a throne, high and lifted up, and his train filled the temple. Above it stood the seraphims: each one had six wings; with twain he covered his face,*

and with twain he covered his feet, and with twain he did fly. And one cried unto another, and said, Holy, holy, holy, is the Lord of hosts: the whole earth is full of his glory. And the posts of the door moved at the voice of him that cried, and the house was filled with smoke. Then said I, Woe is me! For I am undone; because I am a man of unclean lips, and I dwell in the midst of a people of unclean lips: for mine eyes have seen the King, the Lord of hosts. Then flew one of the seraphims unto me, having a live coal in his hand, which he had taken with the tongs from off the altar" (Isaiah 6:1-6)

"And over it the cherubims of glory shadowing the mercy seat; of which we cannot now speak particularly."
(Hebrews 9:5)

"And after these things I saw another angel come down from heaven, having great power; and the earth was lightened with his glory."
(Revelation 18:1)

All three of these scriptures reveal the connection between the angels and the glory. When things are in divine order in our life, ministries, marriages, we will see more activity of angels and more of God's glory manifested.

Zacharias was going in the temple in the order of his course, and the angel came to visit him. He was in divine order.

"And it came to pass, that while he executed

the priest's office before God in the order of his course, according to the custom of the priest's office, his lot was to burn incense when he went into the temple of the Lord. And the whole multitude of the people were praying without at the time of incense. And there appeared unto him an angel of the Lord standing on the right side of the altar of incense," (Luke 1:8-11)

Being in the right place at the right time allows supernatural things to occur in your life and angels are a part of that.

God wants things in divine order in our life, so that the angels can move freely and work fully for us like they are designed to.

"For though I be absent in the flesh, yet am I with you in the spirit, joying and beholding your order, and the stedfastness of your faith in Christ." (Colossians 2:5)

Notice that Paul was rejoicing and commending them with regards to their order.

We are warned not to worship angels. Consider the following:

"Let no man beguile you of your reward in a voluntary humility and worshipping of angels, intruding into those things which he hath not seen, vainly puffed up by his fleshly mind." (Colossians 2:18)

The church in Colossae must have had many visitations to warrant such an instruction. There was divine order and the angels were coming and ministering.

The church at Corinth also understood the necessity of divine order.

> *"But I would have you know, that the head of every man is Christ; and the head of the woman is the man; and the head of Christ is God." (1 Corinthians 11:3)*

The head of every man is Christ. Men, we need to be in submission to Christ, the anointed one and his anointing.

I'm in order when I submit to the Word of God. I submit to what he says to me personally. That's obedience, and in being obedient, I'm dwelling in the secret place under the Most High's shadow.

> *"He that dwelleth in the secret place of the most High shall abide under the shadow of the almighty." (Psalm 91:1)*

When I'm dwelling in the secret place, the angels have charge over me and protect me.

> *"For he shall give his angels charge over thee, to keep thee in all thy ways," (Psalm 91:11)*

There should be order in our families.

> *"Children, obey your parents in the lord: for this is right." (Ephesians 6:1)*

Children are to be submitted by obeying their parents. That is proper order, isn't it?

> *"For this cause ought the woman to have power on her head because of the angels."*
> *(1 Corinthians 11:10)*

She ought to be in proper order because of the angels. Why? Could it be that if your family life is out of order that it would hinder the angels from being able to function fully? In this case, if the woman were not in proper submission with her husband that would hinder the angels much like a man not treating his wife right would hinder his prayers.

> *"Likewise, ye husbands, dwell with them according to knowledge, giving honour unto the wife, as unto the weaker vessel, and as being heirs together of the grace of life; that your prayers be not hindered," (1 Peter 3:7)*

All of us need to be in divine order to be used in ministry. We need to be in divine order for the angels to operate fully with us in the earth.

Chapter Eight

ANGELS TAKE US PLACES

The angels help us many times to get into new places in the spirit.

> *"Behold, I send an angel before thee, to keep thee in the way, and to bring thee into the place which I have prepared."*
> *(Exodus 23:20)*

The angels go and prepare certain spiritual places for us, if we'll let them. The angels help us "stay out" of some places. They help us "get out" of some places. In the Garden of Eden they protected man from getting back in the garden. The angels are involved in helping us to be preserved in the earth and keeping us out of places we shouldn't be.

> *"And the Lord shall deliver me from every evil work, and will preserve me unto his heavenly kingdom..."* *(2 Timothy 4:18)*

In the book of Acts, they're opening doors for the apostles to get out.

> *"But the angel of the Lord by night opened the prison doors, and brought them forth, and said, go, stand and speak in the temple to the people all the words of this life."*
> *(Acts 5:19-20)*

"Peter therefore was kept in prison: but prayer was made without ceasing of the church unto God for him. And when Herod would have brought him forth, the same night Peter was sleeping between two soldiers, bound with two chains; and the keepers before the door kept the prison. And, behold, the angel of the Lord came upon him, and a light shined in the prison: and he smote Peter on the side, and raised him up, saying, Arise up quickly. And his chains fell off from his hands. And the angel said unto him, Gird thyself, and bind on thy sandals. And so he

"AND HIS CHAINS FELL OFF FROM HIS HANDS. AND THE ANGEL SAID UNTO HIM, GIRD THYSELF,..."

did. And he saith unto him, cast thy garment about thee, and follow me. And he went out, and followed him; and wist not that it was true which was by the angel; but thought he saw a vision. When they were past the first and the second ward, they came unto the iron gate that leadeth unto the city; which opened to them of his own accord: and they went out, and passed on through one street; and forthwith the angel departed from him. And when Peter was come to himself, he said, Now I know of a surety, that the Lord hath sent his angel, and hath delivered me out of the hand of Herod, and from all the expectation of the people of the Jews."
(Acts 12:5-11)

Supernatural signs and wonders occur when angels come on the scene to help us. We are going to see more and more of this occur from now on.

Angels also help to bring us into certain places that God has ordained for us.

> *"Behold, I send an Angel before thee, to keep thee in the way, and to bring thee into the place which I have prepared."*
> *(Exodus 23:20)*

If this were true under that covenant, it certainly would be true under the new covenant, a better covenant. God has some things that he wants to bring us into, some places. I'm calling them rooms, spiritual rooms. There are certain places in the spirit that God wants to bring us into for a reason. The angels are trying to help us get there. In the spirit the angels are a part of our inheritance. There's some places in the spirit that we need to get to, and the angels are going to be there with us.

> *"Thus says the Lord of hosts: if you will walk in My ways and keep My charge, then also you shall rule My house and have charge of My courts, and I will give you access* [to My presence] *and places to walk among these who stand here." (Zechariah 3:7 AMP)*

As we are obedient we can all walk in "these places" that are being made known to us - angels are included.

I had an unusual experience in October 1999 in my church. We had a special night of worship and ministry to the Lord. At the end of that service, I wasn't there anymore. I was standing somewhere else, and there was a doorway. As I was looking down, I noticed a threshold. Nobody said anything, but on the inside I felt compelled to step through this doorway. I stepped over, and when I did, there was an angel to my right. He said, "Now you have come into a new room, and you will have to learn to be skillful with the equipment in this room." The next night we had intercessory prayer. As we began to pray in tongues, I got in the spirit again. Every time I closed my eyes, I was in that room. There were different angels and when I would look at them, I would speak in tongues. I could tell by the look on their faces they knew what I was saying, and they were dispatched. I would open my eyes, and be back with every one in the prayer meeting. Then I would close my eyes and be back in that room. The angels want to be more involved in our services, prayer meetings, and ministries.

Here are just a few scriptures to validate visions regarding angelic activity:

> *"There was a certain man in Caesarea called Cornelius, a centurion of the band called the Italian band, a devout man, and one that feared God with all his house, which gave much alms to the people, and prayed to God alway. He saw in a vision evidently about the ninth hour of the day an angel of God coming in to him, and saying unto him, Cornelius. And when he looked on him, he was afraid, and said, what is it, Lord? And he said unto him, Thy prayers and thine alms are come up for a memorial before God. And now send men to Joppa, and call for one Simon, whose surname is Peter: he lodgeth with one Simon a tanner, whose house is by*

the sea side: he shall tell thee what thou oughtest to do." (Acts 10:1-6)

"And now I exhort you to be of good cheer: for there shall be no loss of any man's life among you, but of the ship. For there stood by me this night the angel of God, whose I am, and whom I serve, saying, Fear not, Paul; thou must be brought before Caesar: and, lo, God hath given thee all them that sail with thee. Wherefore, sirs, be of good cheer: for I believe God, that it shall be even as it was told me." (Acts 27:22-25)

"And I Daniel alone saw the vision: for the men that were with me saw not the vision; but a great quaking fell upon them, so that they fled to hide themselves. Therefore I was left alone, and saw this great vision, and there remained no strength in me: for my comeliness was turned in me into corruption, and I retained no strength. Then there came again and touched me one like the appearance of a man, and he strengthened me. And said, O man greatly beloved, fear not: peace be unto thee, be strong, yea, be strong. And when he had spoken unto me, I was strengthened, and said, Let my Lord speak; for thou hast strengthened me." (Daniel 10:7-8, 18-19)

The Lord still speaks to us in visions. All of us will not have visions, but all of us can get in the places that God has ordained for us.

Chapter Nine

OUR AUTHORITY WITH ANGELS

"And Jacob was left alone; and there wrestled a man with him until the breaking of the day. And when he saw that he prevailed not against him, he touched the hollow of his thigh; and the hollow of Jacob's thigh was out of joint, as he wrestled with him. And he said, Let me go, for the day breaketh. And he said, I will not let thee go, except thou bless me. And he said unto him, What is thy name? And he said, Jacob. And he said, Thy name shall be called no more Jacob, but Israel: for as a prince hast thou power with God and with men, and hast prevailed. And Jacob asked him, and said, Tell me, I pray thee, thy name. And he said, Wherefore is it that thou dost ask after my name? And he blessed him there."
(Genesis 32:24-29)

Jacob, as an old covenant man, prevailed with the angel.

"Yea, he had power over the angel, and prevailed: he wept, and made supplication unto him: he found him in Beth-el, and there he spake with us." (Hosea 12:4)

If Jacob had authority with the angel as an old covenant man, how

---

much more do we have authority as believers under the new covenant which is a better covenant.

> *"But now hath he obtained a more excellent ministry, by how much also he is the mediator of a better covenant, which was established upon better promises."*
> *(Hebrews 8:6)*

We need to understand our place of authority as joint heirs with Christ and walk in it daily.

> *"What is man, that thou art mindful of him? And the son of man, that thou visitest him? For thou hast made him a little lower than the angels, and hast crowned him with glory and honour. Thou madest him to have dominion over the works of thy hands: thou hast put all things under his feet,"*
> *(Psalm 8:4-6)*

The scripture in Psalm 8:5 says that God made man a little lower than the angels. The word "angels" is not in the original language at all. The word is "elohim" which is the plural for God. In Genesis 1:26 it says...

> *"...let us (elohim) make man in our image..."*

In reality Psalm 8:5 should read...

> *"...thou hast made him (man) a little lower than God."*

We were created in the image of God.   We were created to be sons and daughters of God. Angels were created as servants.

"Which was the son of Enos, which was the son of Seth, which was the son of Adam, which was the son of God," (Luke 3:38)

"Beloved, now are we the sons of God..." (1 John 3:2a)

In the New Testament, we are "joint heirs with Christ".

"And if children, then heirs; heirs of God, and joint-heirs with Christ; if so be that we suffer with him, that we may be also glorified together." (Romans 8:17)

We are not sub-heirs, but rather joint heirs. My wife and I have a joint bank account, which means we both have equal authority concerning our account. Each of us have the same authority to write checks, deposit, or make withdrawals. In Jesus' name, we now have the same authority as Him.

"Verily, verily, I say unto you, He that believeth on me, the works that I do shall he do also...." (John 14:12a)

When we were born again, we became new creatures and sons of God. We are sharing with Jesus Christ, His authority and His standing.

"Even when we were dead in sins, hath quickened us together with Christ, (by grace ye are saved;) and hath raised us up together, and made us sit together in heavenly places

in Christ Jesus." (Ephesians 2:5-6)

He made us to sit with Him in His authority.

> *"Far above all principality, and power, and might, and dominion, and every name that is named, not only in this world, but also in that which is to come: And hath put all things under his feet, and gave him to be the head over all things to the church, which is his body, the fullness of him that filleth all in all." (Ephesians 1:21-23)*

We are in a position of dominion and authority. All things are under our feet, including angels. We are talking about spiritual authority now that we are in Christ Jesus.

Paul's prayer in this same chapter is for us, as the body, to receive revelation and know who we are in Christ.

> *"That the God of our Lord Jesus Christ, the Father of glory, may give unto you the spirit of wisdom and revelation in the knowledge of him: The eyes of your understanding being enlightened; that ye may know what is the hope of his calling, and what the riches of the glory of his inheritance in the saints, And what is the exceeding greatness of his power to us-ward who believe, according to the working of his mighty power."*
> *(Ephesians 1:17-19)*

We do have authority with angels. They are waiting and listening now.

"Who is gone into heaven, and is on the right hand of God; angels and authorities and powers being made subject unto him."
(1 Peter 3:22)

Angels, authorities and powers are subject to Him and we are joint heirs with Him. We share now with Him in His authority. If angels, authorities, and powers are subject to Him, then they are subject to us also as joint heirs.

The Bible says we shall judge angels.

"Know ye not that we shall judge angels? How much more things that pertain to this life?" *(1 Corinthians 6:3)*

Paul obviously points to a specific future event, however, we do not gain any new spiritual authority after we die. Therefore, we have authority over angels now.

Recently while meditating on this scripture, the word "judge" stood out to me. In thinking of a courtroom, God reminded me that the judge's bench is always elevated. The Lord said the judge is the one with the authority. The Lord then asked me what does the judge do? I said the judge has the authority to confine or release those who stand before him. Then I realized that we are the judges who have authority from God to restrain, restrict, and confine the angels and their activity. We also have authority by our words and covenant to release, liberate, and activate the ministry of angels in the earth.

Chapter Ten

HEALING AND ANGELS

"After this there was a feast of the Jews; and Jesus went up to Jerusalem. Now there is at Jerusalem by the sheep market a pool, which is called in the Hebrew tongue Bethesda, having five porches. In these lay a great multitude of impotent folk, of blind, halt, withered, waiting for the moving of the water. For an angel went down at a certain season into the pool, and troubled the water: whosoever then first after the troubling of the water stepped in was made whole of whatsoever disease he had." (John 5:1-4)

It's evident from this scripture that healing can come with angelic help. We know, on the negative side, evil spirits can cause sickness and disease.

"And it came to pass afterward, that he went throughout every city and village, preaching and shewing the glad tidings of the kingdom of God: and the twelve were with him, and certain women, which had been healed of evil spirits and infirmities, Mary called Magdalene, out of whom went seven devils," (Luke 8:1-2)

It's not strange then that angels, who are spirits, could assist us in

---

ministering healing.

In 1995 I taught eighteen Wednesday nights in a row on the ministry of angels. During all of those services, I laid hands on the sick for healing. A young woman in my church, came forward for ministry, and fell out in the spirit. It's our custom to have someone place what we call a "modesty cloth" over the ladies that fall to the floor during ministry. A cloth was placed over this lady and it covered her from her neck down to almost her knees as she lay on the floor. There was a lot of movement in the center of her body under the cloth. I realized something supernatural was occurring because I could clearly see both her hands stretched out from under the cloth. A few days later, I asked her what had happened. She explained she had female problems and said an angel came and did surgery on her. This is seven years later and she has never had this problem again.

In Honduras I ministered to a lady with a compressed disc. This is her account of the healing; "I felt a hand above and below the affected area of my body. The hands pulled my spine and all the pain left." I asked her how long she had had this problem and she said thirty-six years.

"HE TOLD ME SOMETHING PICKED HIM UP OFF THE FLOOR...AND SOMETHING CAME OUT OF HIS FEET."

In this same meeting a man was in the healing line for ministry concerning allergies. After I ministered to him, he told me something picked him up off the floor as he was standing there and something came out of his feet. He testified that the allergic condition was gone.

Last year while ministering in a city in Southern Indiana, I had a word of knowledge concerning spines. A lady responded with scoliosis of the spine. As I ministered to her, I sensed an angel ministering to her as well. She told me the next night that the angel grabbed her spine at the bottom and pulled it straight.

Two years ago in my home church I felt led to call a young lady forward during a ministry time at the altar. I laid hands on her and proceeded down the altar to minister to others. I quickly turned back in her direction to see an angel pulling something out of her stomach area. I called this young lady at her home that night and related what I had seen at the altar. She told me that she had struggled with anorexia and bulimia for many years and was healed that night and has remained free ever since.

These are just a few of many testimonies we have received concerning angels that were present as we ministered healing and deliverance. I am so glad these ministering spirits are sent to minister to us and for us.

Angelic ministry is received and activated by believing the promises God has given in His Word.

> *"For all the promises of God in him are yea, and in him Amen, unto the glory of God by us," (2 Corinthians 1:20)*

All the promises, including those pertaining to angelic ministry, are yes for those of us who are in Christ Jesus.

Though the Word of God is being taught in many places at this time, many are not accepting their deliverance.

> *"Women received their dead raised to life again: and others were tortured, not*

*accepting deliverance; that they might
obtain a better resurrection,"
(Hebrews 11:35)*

We need to receive from the Father everything he has provided
including deliverance or freedom from the things that are not a
part of our covenant. Sickness, poverty, depression, and worry
are not a part of what He provides. Therefore, refuse to tolerate
them and accept your deliverance from them.

The ministry of an angel delivered the three Hebrews that were
thrown into the fiery furnace.

> *"Then Nebuchadnezzar spake, and said,
> Blessed be the God of Shadrach, Meshach,
> and Abed-nego, who hath sent his angel, and
> delivered his servants that trusted in him, and
> have changed the king's word, and yielded
> their bodies, that they might not serve nor
> worship any god, except their own God,"
> (Daniel 3:28)*

Daniel himself was delivered from the lions den by an angel.

> *"Then said Daniel unto the king, O king,
> live for ever. My God hath sent his angel,
> and hath shut the lions' mouths, that they
> have not hurt me: forasmuch as before him
> innocency was found in me; and also before
> thee, O king, have I done no hurt."
> (Daniel 6:21-22)*

In Acts the apostles were released from prison supernaturally by
an angel.

*"But the angel of the Lord by night opened
the prison doors, and brought them forth..."
(Acts 5:19)*

In all of these cases the people involved accepted their deliverance.
Some, of course, don't know what is available. Then others won't
accept what is available.

I want to receive all that Jesus has redeemed me from. Jesus paid
an awesome price for us to give us our inheritance. Let's continue
to learn what is being offered and be good receivers. Remember
the Word of God that says...

*"Are they not all ministering spirits, sent
forth to minister for them who shall be heirs
of salvation? Therefore we ought to give the
more earnest heed to the things which we
have heard, lest at any time we should let
them slip. For if the Word spoken by angels
was stedfast, and every transgression and
disobedience received a just recompence of
reward; how shall we escape, if we neglect
so great salvation; which at the first began
to be spoken by the Lord, and was confirmed
unto us by them that heard him,"
(Hebrews 1:14 - 2:3)*

This is specifically talking about escaping things on earth through
the ministry of angels. I want to escape everything Jesus said I
could.

What Jesus already paid for in His death, burial, and resurrection,
we are free from. Jesus paid the price with His precious blood, to
free us from sin, sickness, demons and fear. We honor Jesus

when we accept our freedom from these things and take a stand against them.

With angels, as with any Bible subject, we must use our faith for that particular area to be activated. We have a vast inheritance now that we are in Christ Jesus.

> *"In whom also we have obtained an inheritance..." (Ephesians 1:11)*

We are heirs of the new covenant, yet we must mix our faith to cause it to be real in our lives. Once we've heard "the Word" not religion or someone's opinion, then and only then can we have Bible faith for these things.

> *"For unto us was the gospel preached, as well as unto them: but the word preached did not profit them, not being mixed with faith in them that heard it," (Hebrews 4:2)*

Let's be diligent to know our inheritance and receive its benefits.

> *"Are not the angels all ministering spirits (servants) sent out in the service [of God for the assistance] of those who are to inherit salvation?" (Hebrews 1:14 AMP)*

Chapter Eleven

THEY ARE WAITING ON YOU

You and I have the authority to say certain things, which cause the angels to begin to operate with great liberty, or we say things that curtail their ministries and their ability to help us. They want to help us. They have been sent to help us.

Why don't we have more manifestations of angels in our life? If you want angels to manifest themselves, you have to teach about them.

> *"And they went forth and preached every where, the Lord working with them, and confirming the word with signs following."*
> *(Mark 16:20)*

> *"So then faith cometh by hearing, and hearing by the word of God."*
> *(Romans 10:17)*

I've been teaching on angels for over twenty years now. I spent 18 Wednesday nights in a row teaching on angels in 1995. The Word of the Lord came to us in a prophecy saying, "You have created a habitation for the angels." If you don't preach about angels, you are limiting them. They work where the Word is preached about them and believed.

Don't let anything separate you from your covenant. It is a covenant-promise that your angels will have charge over you and keep you all the days of your life. One primary reason things are not happening concerning angelic activity is wrong talking. Your negative confession hinders the angels from their given assignment concerning you. They operate on the Word of God. They hearken to the voice of His Word.

> *"Bless the Lord, ye his angels, that excel in strength, that do his commandments, hearkening unto the voice of his word,"* *(Psalm 103:20)*

The angels are only responsible for activity that is in line with the Bible. You can't charge them contrary to the Bible and have them operate for you.

> *"Suffer not thy mouth to cause thy flesh to sin; neither say thou before the angel, that it was an error: wherefore should God be angry at thy voice, and destroy the work of thine hands?"* *(Ecclesiastes 5:6)*

God is not destroying things, but what it's saying here is that when you talk contrary to the covenant, He is not able to protect you fully like He wants to. Angels are assigned to your children to take care of them and protect them. Sometimes parents don't know anything about this realm. They talk fear, doubt, and unbelief, and it restricts the angels and hinders them. Many tragedies and difficulties could be avoided if parents knew these things and had faith.

> *"My people are destroyed for lack of knowledge: because thou hast rejected knowledge, I will also reject thee, that thou shalt be no priest to me: seeing thou hast*

forgotten the law of thy God, I will also forget thy children." *(Hosea 4:6)*

"For unto us was the gospel preached, as well as unto them: but the word preached did not profit them, not being mixed with faith in them that heard it," *(Hebrews 4:2)*

Sometimes the parents are all messed up and are not living right. Parents sometimes have secret sins. Parents have things going on that nobody else knows, but God knows and the devil knows. Sometimes that can open a door for the enemy to come in. You have to live right and activate your faith in the angels.

"Behold, I send an Angel before thee, to keep thee in the way, and to bring thee into the place which I have prepared. Beware of him, and obey his voice, provoke him not; for he will not pardon your transgressions: for my name is in him. But if thou shalt indeed obey his voice, and do all that I speak; then I will be an enemy unto thine enemies, and an adversary unto thine adversaries. For mine angels shall go before thee, and bring thee in unto the Amorites, and Hittites, and the Perizzites, and the Canaanites, the Hivites, and the Jebusites: and I will cut them off." *(Exodus 23:20-23)*

In other words, you can provoke your angel. I don't want to provoke my angels. Provoke means "to grieve". The angels are grieved when they cannot do what they're designed to do. Which is to help and provide for us. I want them to be able to do everything they've been assigned to do.

One way to provoke your angel is through your words.

"Thou has proved mine heart; thou hast visited me in the night; thou hast tried me, and shalt find nothing; I am purposed that my mouth shall not transgress," (Psalm 17:3)

Their transgression was in the way they spoke. You can talk wrong until you provoke your angel, and he cannot do anything for you. The devil can just come right in and do a lot of things because you have provoked the angels, and they are not able to work for you like they want to.

We've got to put a guard over our mouth, a watch over our tongues, and be careful that we are speaking in line with our covenant of the Word of God.

"Set a watch, O Lord, before my mouth; keep the door of my lips," (Psalm 141:3)

Jesus knew this and he is our example.

"For I have not spoken of myself; but the Father which sent me, he gave me a commandment, which I should say, and what I should speak. And I know that his commandment is life everlasting: Whatsoever I speak therefore, even as the Father said unto me, so I speak," (John 12:49-50)

In only speaking in line with the Word of God and by putting a voice to it, He was assured of angelic ministry and He understood that.

Angels respond to our speech.

> **"Bless the Lord, ye his angels, that excel in strength, that do his commandments, hearkening unto the voice of his word. Bless ye the Lord, all ye his hosts; ye ministers of his, that do his pleasure."**
> **(Psalm 103:20, 21)**

Now let's go back to the latter part of verse 20...

> **"...hearkening unto the voice of his word."**

The word "Voice" means to call aloud, and the word "Word" means to speak, to tell, or "the spoken Word". The angels obey the Word that is spoken out loud.

> **"I will say of the Lord, He is my refuge and my fortress...," (Psalm 91:2)**

> **"Let the redeemed of the Lord say so..."**
> **(Psalm 107:2)**

You need to say something. "Oh, I thank God for the angels." No, that's not going to activate their ministry. You've got to say, "The Lord is my refuge. The Lord is my Fortress. The Lord is my deliverer. He preserves my life. He delivers me from every evil work" (2 Timothy 4:18). When you begin to say the Word of God, the angels begin to hearken. The written Word of God does not have a voice laying on a page in your Bible. You must put your voice to it and speak it out loud.

> **"We having the same spirit of faith, according as it is written, I believed, and**

therefore have I spoken; we also believe, and therefore speak," (2 Corinthians 4:13).

In Psalm 91 the Bible says he charges his angels.

"For he shall give his angels charge over thee, to keep thee in all thy ways."
(Psalm 91:11)

What does that mean? He charges his angels with words. When someone is ordained to a ministry, he or she is charged by speaking particular words to them and over them. God has done the same with the angels. Remember they all have particular ministries or job descriptions.

"Are they not all ministering spirits, sent forth to minister for them who shall be heirs of salvation?" (Hebrews 1:14)

When you begin to speak the same thing in faith to the angels that God has said, that activates their ministries. God has already charged the angels but they're not going to be activated for you until you begin to charge them too.

"Can two walk together, except they be agreed?" (Amos 3:3)

They're not going to be able to fully cooperate in the earth with us until we speak the Word of God. They have ministries, and they want to minister to you and for you.

You've got to pay attention to your words, and you've got to believe the ministering spirits are able to keep you. Part of your inheritance is the ministering spirits that have been sent to minister to you and to your children. We need to charge the angels around us with the right things. We've got to get our words lined up with the Word of God in order to activate their particular ministries in our life.

They're listening for your Words of faith that come out your mouth. Jesus is the high priest of your confession of faith.

> *"Wherefore, holy brethren, partakers of the heavenly calling, consider the Apostle and High Priest of our profession, Christ Jesus,"*
> *(Hebrews 3:1)*

Jesus said...

> *"...whosoever shall confess me, (the Word) before men, him shall the Son of man also confess before the angels of God: but he that denieth me (the Word) before men shall be denied before the angels of God."*
> *(Luke 12:8-9)*

There's something to confessing words of faith or unbelief that's going to release or restrain the ministering spirits. God wants you to speak the Word of God, out of your mouth and believe for their intervention in your life and for your children. You must begin to say, "I am redeemed by the blood of the lamb. I am delivered from every evil work. I am blessed in my coming and going. The Lord shall deliver me from all evil. He will preserve my soul."

You've got to say, "He's given his angels charge over me to keep me in all my ways, and they're guarding me and preserving me. No weapon formed against me will prosper, for I am a servant of God. My righteousness is of you, Father. I thank you Father, you said the angels of God encamp around me because I reverence you, and they deliver me and I agree." When you start saying the Word of God, angels are released, dispatched, and activated, to fulfill and bring to pass the Word of God in your life.

Angels need words to come out of your mouth in faith, based on the words of the covenant. Find out what God says about you and begin to say that. "Father, I thank you that my sufficiency is of you. I thank you, Father, that I can do all things through Christ which strengthens me." In John 12:49, 50, Jesus said...

> *"I only say what my father says, and his Word is life."*

Jesus was saying, "I don't speak death. I don't speak discouragement. I don't speak negatively. I only speak the words of the covenant."

The angel came to Daniel and said...

> *"I came because of your words."*
> *(Daniel 10:12)*

Notice it was Daniel's words that brought the angel. Angels are listening when we pray or when we say. The power of life and death is in your tongue.

> *"Death and life are in the power of the tongue: and they that love it shall eat the fruit thereof," (Proverbs 18:21)*

The angels are listening. This planet is a word planet. It functions and operates by words. God created it that way - it still operates that way.

"In the beginning God created the heaven and the earth. And the earth was without form, and void; and darkness was upon the face of the deep. And the spirit of God moved upon the face of the waters. And God said, let there be light: and there was light. And God saw the light, that it was good: and God divided the light from the darkness,"
(Genesis 1:1-4)

"For verily I say unto you, That whosoever shall say unto this mountain, Be thou removed, and be thou cast into the sea; and shall not doubt in his heart, but shall believe that those things which he saith shall come to pass; he shall have whatsoever he saith"
(Mark 11:23)

There is also another group listening for your words in the spirit too. It's the devil and all of his cohorts under him. This group is full of death, destruction, and anything that steals, kills, and destroys.

"The thief cometh not, but for to steal, and to kill, and to destroy: I am come that they might have life, and that they might have it more abundantly," (John 10:10)

When you speak words contrary to the covenant you give this group a legal right. This allows them to enforce their plans.

"Lest Satan should get an advantage of us: for we are not ignorant of his devices."
(2 Corinthians 2:11)

"He shutteth his eyes to devise froward things: moving his lips he bringeth evil to pass." (Proverbs 16:30)

You can talk wrong until "you" bring evil to pass.

"...Neither say thou before the angel, that it was a error: wherefore should God be angry at thy voice..." (Ecclesiastes 5:6)

Do you know God can get angry at what you say sometimes? James said you could deceive your own heart by the words of your mouth.

"If any man among you seem to be religious, and bridleth not his tongue, but deceiveth his own heart, this man's religion is vain," (James 1:26)

You have to learn to talk correctly, like a covenant person.

"The heart of the wise teacheth his mouth, and addeth learning to his lips," (Proverbs 16:23)

I heard Brother Copeland say that the angels are preprogrammed. In my study of angels over the last twenty years, what he said made sense to me. I began to think about the angels being preprogrammed, and I realized a connection between activating the angels and some of our technology. The Bible says He charges His angels with the Word of God. When you begin to speak the Word of God in faith, that activates the angels. What you say has to be the words that they are already charged or programmed with.

I got a new car and it had a little computer chip in the sun visor. The salesman at the lot said, "Now when you get home, take your remote control for the garage, put it up next to the visor, push the button in, a light will come on and it will click, click, click. When it stops clicking, turn loose of it and the chip is programmed to open your garage door. I put the garage door remote in a drawer somewhere after that. I just push that little device on my visor now. What I'm saying to you is this, the garage door opener and the device in my visor are both charged with the same instructions. When I hit it, the door automatically opens.

God has charged the angels with his Word and when we charge them with the same instructions then we activate their function. They're not going to be able to fully cooperate in the earth with us until we speak the Word of God. They have ministries, and they want to minister not only to you, but also for you. Remember that they are waiting on you.

ABOUT THE AUTHOR

Michael P. Jacobs is founding pastor of Church on the Rock in New Albany, Indiana and has been in ministry for over 30 years. Along with authoring several books, including *Spiritual Father or Spiritual Failure*, he currently serves as a board member of Dr. Ed Dufresne's "Fresh Oil Fellowship." A pastor to several pastors and missionaries, Pastor Jacobs has ministered on more than 70 mission trips and travels extensively throughout the United States ministering the Word of God. Physical healings, deliverance, and a tangible anointing are evident in his meetings. His wife, Diana, his daughter and son-in-law, Jessica and Jacob, and his son Jordan are also involved with him in the ministry.

If you would like to contact the author, please write:

Church on the Rock
Attn: Michael P. Jacobs
4224 Mel Smith Road
New Albany, Indiana 47150

or call:
(812) 948-5906

or e-mail:
cotr@insightbb.com

Please include your testimony or help received from this book when you write.

ADDITIONAL MATERIALS

MICHAEL JACOBS MINISTRIES   *(Available in Spanish*)*

BOOKS:
Angels on Earth: They are Waiting on You*
Spiritual Father or Spiritual Failure*

DVD MATERIALS:

Angels on Earth	Faith Rewards Program
Healing 101 Honor*	Hope
Impartations	Ministering Spirits and Healing
Refreshed and Redeemed*	Shaping Your Destiny
Special Endowments	Spiritual Father or Spiritual Failure
Words Have Seasons	Words Release Your Faith

COMPACT DISC MATERIALS:

Angels on Earth Series	Angels Take Us Places
Faith Has a Voice	Fellowshiping with the Father
Gold, Guys/Girls & the Glory	Healing is God's Will
Job and Paul's Thorn	Man's Authority Restored
Ministering Spirits and Money	Spiritual Fathers
Stay With It	Your Future is in Your Mouth
You Have to Say It	Your Supply is Here